I've Got to Comb My Hair

A Memoir

By
Shawnte M. Mckinnon

©Shawnte Mckinnon

All rights reserved. No part of this publication may be reproduced in any form; electronic or mechanical, including scanning, photocopying or any information storage or retrieval system without the prior written consent of copyright holder.

I'VE GOT TO COMB MY HAIR

I'VE GOT TO COMB MY HAIR

Acknowledgements

I have to give honor to God who is the head and savior of my life. Without the leading and guidance of the Holy Spirit, this would not be possible. God is the author and finisher of my story. I want to thank my parents, Frederick and Tresa Yon Gainer and Carol Mckinnon for always believing in me; your support gave me that extra push needed to complete this book. I would also like to thank my fans, my siblings...I thank you guys for seeing the best in your sister. In addition, I have to thank God for all the Godly Warriors he brought into my life who were always on the sidelines praying and interceding for me through the journey of writing this book; La'Tivia, Rhonda, Nicole, Donine, Lucretia, Ruth, Germaine, Edna and so many others. You guys rock!! I am so blessed to have each of you in my life. I would be remiss if I did not mention my Aunts Jannie McCluster and Lula Jones, Cousins, David and Jean Perry and Kimberly Thorne; you guys have always been there when I needed you!! Thank you all so much!!

DEDICATION

*This book is dedicated in loving memories of my grandmothers, the late **Essie M Gainer** and **Inez Trammel- Martin***

It was your love and dedication that brought me through!

I'VE GOT TO COMB MY HAIR

FOREWARD

Shawnte Monique McKinnon is a minister of the Gospel, prolific speaker, powerful prayer warrior, entrepreneur, radio talk show host and extraordinary woman of God who has overcome many major personal struggles in her lifetime. While having the pleasure of knowing Prophetess McKinnon only a matter of a few years, we have become kindred spirits and it feels as if we have known each other for years. Prophetess McKinnon has a sincere passion for God's people, specifically those who have been hurt and are in need of healing. God has graced her with a special anointing to speak life and wholeness to a dying world and even though she is currently battling multiple sclerosis, she always finds the strength to communicate the love of Christ to those in need of encouragement. Overcoming a painful past, trial and tribulation, domestic violence, personal tragedy, the naysayers and quite often misunderstood, Prophetess McKinnon has risen like a phoenix out of the ashes and has put pen to paper to minister to the masses with this heartfelt piece pouring out of her soul as only she can. I would ask that you sit back and enjoy as she walks you through a snippet of her youth. You will laugh, you will cry, you will encounter the essence of the Prophetess in her first of many works. So I introduce to some and present to others the Minister, the author, the Prophetess, Shawnte Monique McKinnon.

Germaine M. Anderson, Ambassador of the Most High

I'VE GOT TO COMB MY HAIR

TABLE OF CONTENTS

CHAPTER 1-SUMMER TRIP   9

CHAPTER 2-BACK HOME   22

CHAPTER 3-FAILURE IS NOT AN OPTION   43

CHAPTER 4-I'VE GOT TO COMB MY HAIR   55

CHAPTER 5-TRANSITION   87

CHAPTER 6-THE STRUGGLE   103

CHAPTER 7-LIFE LESSONS   112

I'VE GOT TO COMB MY HAIR

I'VE GOT TO COMB MY HAIR

SUMMER TRIP

"Brian come downstairs!!" My mother was calling for my oldest brother to come downstairs because we were on our way to Florida to visit my grandmother for the summer. My brother yelled back, "Nooo", from behind a locked bathroom door.

The negotiating process between my brother and mom went on for about 20 minutes. He obviously did not want to go to Florida. My siblings and I lived with my parents in Brooklyn, NY in a two story apartment.

Waking up and going to sleep every day to loud music, the sound of ambulances, police cars, and the smell of fried plantains and pizza parlors were the norm. It was the city life. It was just three of us at the time which consisted of my eldest brother, sister and me; I was the baby.

My brother didn't come out of the bathroom and my mother gave up trying to get him out; so only my sister and I ended up traveling to Florida. My memory of the day was quite vague, but it was the day that life, as I had known it, was about to change.

I'VE GOT TO COMB MY HAIR

I don't know how I got to the car, but I remember somehow being in the car with my Aunt, my dad's sister, and her husband along with my older sister. I was three years old at the time and this was my first time traveling far without my parents. Though I didn't know what to expect, I couldn't stop the uneasy feeling I was having in the pit of my little stomach; suddenly the lights went out in my mind and I was drifting off to sleep.

When I awakened after a long sleep, I woke up in a strange house, one that I was not familiar with. There was an older lady in the room smiling at me and I had no idea who she was. I began to cry and as the tears flowed down my face, I looked around in search for my mom or my dad, but they were nowhere to be found.

The old lady tried to console me and tell me everything was going to be alright, but truthfully, I had never seen someone so old in person before and she actually scared me. I quickly learned that the older woman was my great grandmother. She was my father's grandmother and everyone called her "Mama".

I'VE GOT TO COMB MY HAIR

Mama lived in a small, quaint house with big wooden doors that led to other rooms with wooden doors and neatly made beds; every artifact had its own distinct place. Mama's house often smelled of baked macaroni and cheese, cornbread, collard greens, baked apples, and baked chicken. You would find her in the kitchen cooking, baking, and singing in the wee hours of the morning. She had somewhat of a rusty high pitched voice and every morning you would hear her bellow out in that rusty voice, *"Don't let his name go down, Oh, don't let his name go down."* Mama was singing about the Lord and she didn't seem to mind that she did not have the best singing voice.

Mama was a medium brown skin woman who wore glasses. She had gray hair that she rolled religiously every night with those pink sponge rollers. She was a strict woman and it appeared that she had a permanent scowl on her face, even when she smiled. As time progressed, I learned a lot about Mama because my summer trip turned into 11 years.

I ended up living with my grandmother Essie, who we fondly called "Madea". My grandmother was a soft spoken woman who always seemed frustrated. We lived in a small town next door to Mama. The towns were divided by a two mile bridge that my grandmother seemed always nervous to drive over, she did it, but not without telling us to be quiet first. The town had one grocery store, one stop light, one elementary and one high school. It was a town with houses that had manicured lawns and where no one was really a stranger; everybody knew everybody. It was certainly different from the place that I once knew as my home.

    My great grandmother and great aunt had a hand in helping my grandmother raise my sister and me. Those three women were avid church goers and we hardly ever missed a church service. They lived under the strict principles of religion and ruled their homes as such. Children were to be seen, but not heard.

    My grandmother attended a Pentecostal church, back then we called it 'holiness church'…. I remember entering in an old school house that they were using as a church. Everything inside looked brown, the pews were made up of brown benches and the floors were old wooden brown floors. The pulpit and the choir stand were brown and the lights were dim, but I guess that was due to the dirty glass covers on the old light fixtures.

The bathroom was outside of the church and I would be afraid to use it if we had night service, but my grandmother would take me out and assure me she was looking out for me as I would squat with my little legs trying not to have an accident on myself. My grandmother would pass me tissue that she carried in her purse because there was no tissue out there. She never left home without tissue and peppermint in her purse and we had to make sure we did the same or she would have a fit.

I remember watching the Pastor pray for people at the altar; I guess this was some type of revival. The Pastor looked as though he was towering over the people in his white robe that covered his plumped body. He would take white towels and draw a cross on the towel with anointed oil that had red dye in it.

I watched as he would place these towels over people's head and wave his hands praying something I really couldn't quite make out at the time. Some people would fall out, break out in a dance, and others would shake uncontrollably because they had the Holy Ghost. It was my first time seeing something like this. I would hide behind the pews and peek through the wooden slat benches, watching, hoping no one would notice me because I was afraid of the 'ghost'.

At home, Madea yelled and screamed a lot, but in my opinion, she never screamed or yelled at the right people. She seem to direct her frustrations on people who would take it from her whether that was by choice or not; however, she believed in God and wanted everybody to be saved and she was going to make sure of it.

Every service the pastor would make an open invitation of salvation to the attendees. My grandmother would beckon for me to go to the altar. I would go up to the altar and have to call on Jesus. This was known as tarry service.

The mothers of the church (which consisted of a group of older ladies) would stand behind me cheering me on as if I was getting ready to make a touchdown in football. They would say, "*Call em baby, call em*". I would be down on my knees calling out the name "Jesus" repetitively. Being down on my knees felt like an eternity. I would begin crying and half stating the name "*Jesus*" and the mothers rejoiced. They thought Jesus had finally come down to save my soul, but I just really wanted to get up off my knees. **Proverbs 22:6 states, Train up a child in the way he should go: and when he is old, he will not depart from it.**

    My life as a child was certainly an interesting one… full of pain, confusion, and sometimes joy. I would always reminisce about my parents and my family in New York. I would constantly recite my memories of my Mom, Dad, and older brother over dinner with my great grandmother.

    I'm not sure if she was interested, but she would let me tell my story anyway. These memories kept me alive and gave me hope that one day I would be reunited with my parents. The elders in my family were very secretive about my parents and the reasoning of why we were now living in Florida. I learned quickly not to ask too many questions, because an inquisitive child was considered too grown for their own good and "A child must stay in a child's place". My great grandmother would let us know this without hesitation.

My sister spent our first few years in Florida living with my great aunt and I lived with my grandmother Madea. I'm not sure why we were separated, but I enjoyed seeing my sister when my grandmother would drop me off in Sneads where my great grandmother and great aunt lived.

I absolutely dreaded going to Mama's house. Mama did not believe in sparing the rod and I got the rod almost every time I visited. Mama and I never really understood each other. LOL!! I was a very outgoing-outspoken child, but mama thought I talked too much and was way too grown. She used to say in that rusty voice and a southern drawl, "I mean that Shawwwnnntaynnnee is dangerous!" LOL!! Mama could not pronounce my name properly. LOL!! I remember times just walking into mama's house and speaking and she would find a reason to whack me. LOL!! I laugh today, but back then it wasn't funny.

I'VE GOT TO COMB MY HAIR

I just really tried to stay on her good side, but that was a very difficult thing to do. When Mama got mad, she would say "*You'll never amount to anything*". I never let what she said get me down. I would just look at her thinking, *I'll show you*. Looking back on it, it was almost as if she was determined to break my spirit.

Mama came from a generation where blacks worked in the cotton field and the "White Man's" homes to provide for their families. She grew up in a time of segregation and hard labor. She could not relate to children who did not understand those times.

My sister and I would laugh and play like normal kids, but mama would make us stop laughing. She would point her finger at us and say "Stop all that laughing, the white man is going to think you're stupid." Due to the fact that we didn't grow up in that era, we did not understand what she meant by that statement. I really thought she was losing her mind.

My childhood was a very challenging one as there was a huge generational gap between the elders and me. My grandmother didn't believe in taking us to the movies, ball games, or parties. She was a 'holiness woman' and 'holiness women' did not allow their children to participate in those kinds of things, because it was considered sinful. Needless to say, I missed out on a lot of childhood fun.

My grandmother would take me to the circus and she would let me go to the fair if someone she trusted was going. I always felt so naïve and so behind because my life was so sheltered. I didn't know all the childhood games or songs; however, I would learn some stuff from my peers in school. Eventually we got a chance to attend dances and games, but not without much hesitation from my grandmother and a little rebellion from us.

My sister and I spent most of our time at church events. We had to attend vacation bible school every summer, which I hated. I wanted to go on a real vacation like Disney World. I never went to Disney World as a child and I lived in the State of Florida. When I would ask my grandmother about going to these places, she would say "I'm just your grandmother; your parents would have to take you." I really thought that was an interesting response, because I didn't know when I would see or speak to my parents again.

My mom came to visit when I was six years old. She just had my baby brother, her second son. I was so excited to see her as I had not seen her since I left New York. I clung to my mother while she was there as a child in my situation would do, but my elders reminded me, Mama in particular, that I was still in their care.

My mother's visit was short lived and while I was away at school, she left and went back to New York. I was broken hearted. I remember breaking down crying not understanding why she left me, us… in Florida. Many questions ran through my head that day. The elders in my family weren't very nurturing so no one comforted me in my pain. The topic of my parents was always so hush hush and I assumed this was their way of protecting us.

I learned to comfort my pain through my prayers. My grandmother taught me how to pray and I would always pray that God protect my mommy and daddy; however, I would always say a silent prayer to return home to them. About two years later, my dad came to Florida and lived with us for a while. I heard whispers from the elders about why my dad was coming to stay with us, but I was too young to truly understand what I was hearing.

I remember my grandmother taking my Dad around to look for houses. My mother was still living in New York at the time and was pregnant with her fifth child, my third brother. I enjoyed my dad being there and I wanted to stay as close to him as possible.

He even taught me how to ride my bike and my own theme song. I would go to school and recite it often while my classmates would do background beats on the desk for me. I would stand up in the middle of my classmates rapping "*My name is Shawnte and that's ok. I got class and finesse, that's what people say. I've been known in the east, I've been known in the west. Sucker MC's try to copy my test. Hoa!*" I was the cool kid with my own song. Lol!!

I thought my parents were going to move to Florida and we would be a family again. Unfortunately, this never happened. My parents had parted ways and my father moved down south to Ft. Lauderdale where he began his new life with his new wife. My sister and I continued to stay with our grandmother, but still no explanation from the adults as to why we were there.

I remember being so hurt seeing my father packing his things and leaving. I wondered why he would not take me with him. Once again, I found myself having to pick up the pieces of my little emotions and re-adapting to the life that was chosen for me. My dad and step mom would come for periodic visits and take us shopping and out to eat.

I enjoyed hanging out with my dad. He would also send clothes and shoes for school and different church events. The kids at school would rave over our outfits because they were always so different. One kid asked, "Is your dad a drug dealer?" Those questions really didn't offend me much, but I made sure to let out a "*Hell no*" to set the record straight. Of course this was out of the presence of adults. I'm sure if my grandmother knew I was cursing, I would have been met with a guaranteed beat down!

I'VE GOT TO COMB MY HAIR

BACK HOME

    I was 11 years old when I took my first trip back to the place I once knew as home. My father and my step mother drove up from Ft. Lauderdale to pick us up. The two of them took turns driving along with my dad's first cousin, who we called Dock. Dock is his nickname. It was an 18 hour drive and I was stuck sitting uncomfortably in the middle between my sister and whoever was not driving or in the passenger's seat at the time. I had this feeling of excitement in my stomach.

    I couldn't wait to see my family, especially my mom and brothers. By this time, my mom had another baby- another boy. It wasn't much I knew about my mother's current life as I was not in contact with her very often, but I was very excited to see her.

    We arrived at Grandma's apartment in Harlem. Grandma is my mom's mother, who lived on the 23rd floor of her building. The city life was still pretty much the same as I had remembered it. You can hear loud music coming from the windows. I smelled food coming from the different apartments and surrounding restaurants, in addition, the smoke coming out the gas exhaust from the buses and cars filled the air as they were zooming by in the busy streets of New York.

Once entering grandma's building, I smelled the familiar scent of urine from people who did not take the time to go inside to use the restroom. Yes, I was back home. I could not believe it. I had prayed many nights and years to see this day and it was finally here.

My dad knocked on grandma's door, an unfamiliar voice answered, "*Who is it?*" I didn't recognize the voice. I asked my dad, "*Who is that?*" Dad responded by saying his name. He said, "*Its Cody*" and then looks down at me and said "*Oh, that's your grandfather's son.*" I was confused at this point, but I learned much after entering into the apartment.

The man I know as my grandfather is my mom's stepfather and the only grandfather, I knew on my mom's side. My younger siblings refer to him as Poppy, which took me a long time to get used to because I only knew him by his first name. I never knew my grandfather had a son, but I was about to meet his son for the first time.

When the door opened, we were met with lots of hugs and kisses from my grandparents. I was so happy to see my older brother as I had not seen him in years. I really missed him. We were all pretty close from what I could remember, although he used to do all kinds of mischievous things to us that an older brother would do- like ripping the head off of our baby dolls and shocking our tongues with cords that he pulled out of an electrical outlet….smh! Nonetheless, we loved our big brother!

I got a chance to hug all three of my younger brothers as well. They were quite shy and had the giggles. The youngest of us all was still a baby in diapers. He was just the cutest baby with lots of hair. I loved being there with my siblings.

My dad left us there to spend time with our siblings and grandparents. My mom's sister and her husband also came to see us and we spent time at their apartment as well. My aunt took us school shopping and we had a great time! I kept asking for my mom and they told me she will be coming to visit soon. I remember feeling like a fish out of a pond, even though New York was my home, I left at such a young age and was raised in a small town that I felt a little overwhelmed by the busyness of the city.

    My mom came to visit and she was quite different from what I remember. She was wearing a scarf around her head and her stomach was bulging. She was pregnant again, but this time it was a girl. When she came to the door, I ran yelling mommy into her arms. My sister followed suit. I quickly notice that there was something different about my mother, but I could not quite put my finger on it; however, I would soon find out what made my mother different from what I remember her to be.

    My mother's demeanor was quite solemn. Although she was still beautiful as I had remembered her to be, her attire was different. She wore a short sundress with tennis shoes. The scarf on her head threw me off as well. My mother was somewhat of a fashionista and this was not her norm.

I'VE GOT TO COMB MY HAIR

I couldn't really gage if she was happy to see us or not. She didn't have that same cheerful smile that I remembered. She hugged us, but she was very distant- almost as if her mind was in another place. I brushed it off, but I was puzzled; it had been five years since I last saw her.

My sister and I spent some time with our relatives in New York. We traveled from borough to borough visiting all of our family. It was a great experience, but I also learned some not so good news…. My mother was struggling with substance abuse. Both she and my father had a bout with it, but this was kept secret from us.

My father had gotten himself clean and moved on with his life and my mother was working on kicking the habit. I remember returning back to Florida thinking to myself, why didn't anyone tell me. I asked my grandmother why I was not told this about my parents, she responded, "*I wanted you all to find out on your own.*" I guess she was trying to protect us from the painful news.

My grandmother and I did not discuss what I learned anymore after that day. After our

I'VE GOT TO COMB MY HAIR

first visit to New York, we visited a couple more times during the summer. It wasn't until I was 14 years old that life took another major turn for me.

My sister lost her high school sweetheart to a car accident. My grandmother was concerned about her well-being and thought that it was best she returned to New York with my parents. My father along with his wife had moved back to New York by this time. My mom, who was now drug free at this time, came to pick her up and take her back to New York. I stayed behind.

I had to go to summer school that year because my math teacher threatened to send me if I did not turn in my math book. Well, I let another student borrow my book and when I asked for it back, he acted as if he had amnesia. As promised by my math teacher, I ended up in summer school. I thought my grandmother was going to kill me for having to go, but she let it slide. Although I had never been to summer school before and dreaded going, it turned out to be a not so bad experience as I was able to make a lot of new friends.

I'VE GOT TO COMB MY HAIR

One day while coming home from school, my grandmother decided to tell me she was sending me back to New York as well. I immediately begin to cry and ask her why. She said it was time for me to go back home to be with my parents. I told her I didn't want to go. She said, "*I need you to look after your sister.*" My sister was older than me, but I think my grandmother used me as her guardian angel to make sure she did not get into any trouble. My grandmother and I both sat in the car and cried that day.

I found myself back in New York for good at the age of 14. I remember being in my mom's 17th floor apartment looking out the window wondering what would life be like for me back in the big apple. So many things were different now as both my parents had remarried and my mom had more children. I was the baby when I left; now I was the third eldest out of seven children.

I called my childhood friend in Florida to let her know that I will not be returning to Florida after the summer. I think this was another day that I will never forget. She was my best friend; we had been friends since the first grade. When I gave her the news, she began to cry and of course my tears begin to follow. I told her we would stay in touch, which we in fact did.

New York proved itself to be a challenge. There was so much hurt, pain, and resentment that peaked its head every time there was an opportunity with my family. I lived with my dad and stepmother as my mother and I did not see eye to eye, and I absolutely did not care for the man she married. He was still battling drug abuse. I had lived such a sheltered life with my grandmother in Florida and I refused to tolerate any chaos if I could help it.

I somewhat tried to keep my life as normal as possible, even though life had drastically changed for me. I was no longer living in the confines of a Christian moral home, but with a dad who did not go to church nor believed in Christianity itself. I would often smell weed coming from his room. Yes, things were certainly different.

My mother's husband was a thief and he would steal your underwear if he could make some money off of it to buy drugs. I got into

I'VE GOT TO COMB MY HAIR

many arguments with my mother about him. If I stayed at her house, I would sleep with my clothes and jewelry on and kept my bags nearby. You had to always be on guard with him around. I did not trust him as there was something very dark and evil about him.

My mother's husband was like an everyday chore for her I guess; she was always so focused on his whereabouts and what he was doing. I felt she didn't have much time for me and I resented her for it. I could not understand why would someone who had not been in their child's life for years not take the opportunity to do so when it was presented to them. When I would address it, she would quickly tell me that he was her man and I did not have to deal with her man. I resented her even more when she would make such statements to me.

My dad and I had our struggles too; however, I was able to tolerate him a little better. Nonetheless, I was glad to not have to worry about my clothes being stolen or being ignored by my dad. My dad and I would get into arguments that would turn into some vicious cursing matches. It pained me that we would speak to each other that way as I had never uttered a curse word in front of my grandmother.

    In New York, I always felt like I was on the defense and I had to defend myself from what I considered destructive lifestyles. I quickly realized that my parents weren't the parents I had remembered and this would be an uphill battle.

    I became a cheerleader and kept myself engrossed in school activities to drown out the problems at home. I attended Dewitt Clinton my sophomore year and half of my junior year of high school in the Bronx where we lived. I met my new best friend, Shawn, on the cheerleading team. Little did Shawn know, she and her family was such a blessing to me during my years in New York. I spent much time at their house eating, watching movies, and sharing girl stories. LOL!! It was my place of refuge away from the chaos I experienced at home. It was very rare for me to stay home. I stayed wherever I could find peace.

    We ended up moving to Queens. I decided that I would not join the cheerleading team at my new school as I felt loyal to the team in the Bronx. I met my other high school bestie, Annette, at this new school. Annette and I spent our time getting our hair, nails and eyebrows done. We loved shopping and going to the store to buy Deuce Deuce and Heinekens.

We were too young to drink, but it didn't stop us from going into the corner store and purchasing drinks. Of course, we hid this from our parents. Annette was my other outlet from home. We hopped on the train and rode all over New York, without a care in the world. I also spent a lot of time with my older cousins, on my father's side of the family, who always looked after me like I was their little sister.

I found myself creating normalcies to function. I would even attend church with some of my father's relatives. I was the only one in my house that would attend church. Every Sunday they would come pick me up for church. My dad would yell out to me as I was on my way out the door saying, *and don't give that pimp all your money.* Smh!! The pimp my dad was referring to was the preacher.

I'VE GOT TO COMB MY HAIR

He did not believe in going to church; however, his beliefs didn't move my beliefs at all. If I didn't know anything else, I knew I needed God. This was something my grandmother instilled in me. Even my high school boyfriend, who was a five percenter (they believe a percentage of the bible and the Koran), challenged me on why I went to church. He would say, "*You go in there every Sunday, do the Charleston* (shouting in the Holy Ghost)*, and come out and the world is still the same.*" I didn't care what anyone thought about my beliefs, I knew only God could truly help me.

I often felt like I was going to lose my mind in New York. I would call my grandmother and tell her these people up here are crazy. I said this is like some real life Jerry Springer show. She would tell me that God would work it out and that she was praying. When I tell you that was the last thing I wanted to hear, that was the last thing I wanted to hear. I really wanted my life to go back to the life as I had known it. Once again, I felt like the adults made decisions without truly considering us, from my perspective.

I had to watch my two younger brothers as my dad had custody of them. This irritated me because I had a lot of responsibility with them. My dad and my stepmother both worked at night and the responsibility for caring for them fell into my lap. I had to cook for them, help them with their homework, pick out their clothes for school, and make sure they had their bath. It was a bit much for a young teenager who never had this kind of responsibility before. In addition to taking care of them, I had to make sure my work was done as well. I was angry all the time. I thought my parents were irresponsible and inconsiderate. I had to grow up and grow up quickly.

There were many fights with my parents. My dad and I got into such a bad argument that it turned into a fist fight. I never thought in a million years that I would end up in a fight with my dad! I argued with my mom all the time. I struggled with respecting my parents. I really didn't know how to take them and they did not know how to take me.

I'VE GOT TO COMB MY HAIR

Our lives were different. I fought for my sanity daily and daily I thought I was losing it. I tried to distance myself from my parents as much as possible. It appeared that my mom hated when I came over because me and her husband were sure to argue. He was so disrespectful to not only my mom, but also towards her children. I could never understand why she would take it; it made me angry.

I would curse her husband out if he blinked wrong which caused my mom to intervene often. I made sure to drop a few 'f' bombs when I wanted him to understand what I would do to him if he got out of line in my presence. I knew my dad would kill him if he tried to 'pop' off on me. I felt he was the reason my mom and I didn't have a relationship.

I stayed with my mom a few days when I decided to leave home and I went on strike from my dad. Before my school and my brothers' school were changed, I was still traveling with them to the Bronx and taking them to school. This was a cumbersome task for me. I would wake up early to get myself and brothers ready for school.

We had to be out the house by 5 a.m. to get to school on time. They were still very young and would be so tired. There would be times that the trains would be so jam packed that we would have to stand up. I would let my brothers lean on me to sleep in the mornings. My father refused to change their schools so I moved out and refused to take them to school. It forced him to change their schools to Queens.

While my dad and I did not always see eye to eye, he would often impart little nuggets of wisdom along the way. My father would have these conversations with me that I always kept in my back pocket; they became useful as the years progressed.

He said, "*Shawnte remember this, you can be the prettiest girl in the room, but one day someone will come in prettier than you. You may be the fastest runner, but one day someone will out run you; however, none of that matters, all you have to do is be the best you that you can be.*" One of my favorite quotes from my father went something like this, "*The world is a teacher and you are a student, as long as you recognize that you are learning you will become much wiser. However, if you feel like a victim, then you will always be preyed upon."* These nuggets taught me a lot.

We lived in a two family house in Queens. We lived on the top floor and our landlord lived on the bottom floor. They were fairly new and quite nice apartments. Our landlord was a single Jamaican guy in his thirties. He was a pervert. This grown man did not hide his attraction towards me. I was always very watchful of him.

He was always making slick comments and would offer me rides when he saw me walking by myself. I would decline. There was no way I was getting in the car with him by myself. He would solicit sex from prostitutes and I could hear him late at night attacking them because he didn't want to pay for their services. I would wake up in the middle of the night to loud screams and thumps; my bedroom was over the entrance to our home.

One day while me and my boyfriend was sitting on the steps in front of the house, this prostitute came up asking us if we knew the man that live downstairs, we told her yes. She said, *"Well tell him he ain't getting no pu**y from me for no five dollars"*. I was in complete shock, but anything is possible in New York. My boyfriend could not wait to tell the landlord what the prostitute said, because he wanted to humiliate him. Shortly after the prostitute left, my landlord pulled up in the driveway in his BMW and my boyfriend without hesitation said, *"Yo Albert, this prostitute just stopped by and said you ain't getting no pu**y from her for no five dollars."*

    My boyfriend and I busted out laughing. The look on my landlord's face was priceless. He was so embarrassed. He replied back in a stutter saying, *"Oh…um...Next time a stranger come up here like that you guys should call the police."* I began thinking, *I should call the police on you when I hear you attacking them at night.*

    I was 17 years old at this time when I started dating. I guess I fell into the statistic of good girls liking bad boys, because my high school boyfriend was certainly rough around the edges. He had that inner nerd in him that he only seem to let out when he was around me, but outside of that he was a thug. I always felt safe when he was around because my landlord knew he was not the type to be messed with.

There was never a dull moment in New York, but there were many days I hoped for one peaceful moment. These experiences built endurance and strength I did not know I had. I had a fire and feistiness like no other, but I had no choice. I carried a box cutter with me at all times and my mouth was a box cutter by itself, but just in case I needed back up, the physical cutter was in my purse. It was live or die trying.

Speaking of protection, the prayers my grandmother taught me came in handy in addition to the bible she gave me. My bible was like ID, I didn't leave home without it. I would read the 91st Psalms at night as my grandmother suggested:

He that dwelleth in the secret place of the most High shall abide under the shadow of the Almighty.

I'VE GOT TO COMB MY HAIR

² I will say of the Lord, He is my refuge and my fortress: my God; in him will I trust.

³ Surely he shall deliver thee from the snare of the fowler, and from the noisome pestilence.

⁴ He shall cover thee with his feathers, and under his wings shalt thou trust: his truth shall be thy shield and buckler.

⁵ Thou shalt not be afraid for the terror by night; nor for the arrow that flieth by day;

⁶ Nor for the pestilence that walketh in darkness; nor for the destruction that wasteth at noonday.

⁷ A thousand shall fall at thy side, and ten thousand at thy right hand; but it shall not come nigh thee.

⁸ Only with thine eyes shalt thou behold and see the reward of the wicked.

⁹ Because thou hast made the Lord, which is my refuge, even the most High, thy habitation;

¹⁰ There shall no evil befall thee, neither shall any plague come nigh thy dwelling.

¹¹ For he shall give his angels charge over thee, to keep thee in all thy ways.

¹² They shall bear thee up in their hands, lest thou dash thy foot against a stone.

> **¹³ Thou shalt tread upon the lion and adder: the young lion and the dragon shalt thou trample under feet.**
> **¹⁴ Because he hath set his love upon me, therefore will I deliver him: I will set him on high, because he hath known my name.**
> **¹⁵ He shall call upon me, and I will answer him: I will be with him in trouble; I will deliver him, and honour him.**
> **¹⁶ With long life will I satisfy him, and shew him my salvation."**

I only had the King James Version of the bible at the time and really didn't understand what it fully meant, but I knew it was my protection.

    I often questioned God about why my life had to be the way that it was. Faith was instilled in me at a young age. God would allow my mind to travel back to the times where I would make a request in my prayer to return home. I was now back at home and did not want to be there. I learned a valuable lesson in the process and that was to be careful for what you pray for…

I'VE GOT TO COMB MY HAIR

FAILURE IS NOT AN OPTION

One of my biggest fears in life was failing. I struggled my senior year of high school, but I was determined to graduate. Most of my intermediate family did not complete high school, but some got their GED.

I decided that getting out of school was a must. I pushed through and graduated while still facing many obstacles. I was the first to get a high school diploma in my intermediate family. I was so angry with my parents at the time; I did not even go to my own graduation or tell them I graduated.

I remember my dad and I got into a heated argument and he said, "*I don't even know if you finished school.*" I was so offended by his comment that I went in my room, grabbed my diploma and threw it at him. I ended up leaving the house as I would normally do when I got angry.

I spent my teens running, trying to find peace. If I didn't know anything else, I knew how to leave. While in New York, I had become a little more adventurous. Me and my best friend Annette loved hanging out in Greenwich

I'VE GOT TO COMB MY HAIR

Village better known as the Village in New York.

    I think hanging out down there influenced some of our decisions. We loved shopping, eating, and clubbing in the village, but the village introduced us to other things like piercings and tattoos. One day while hanging out in the village I told Annette I wanted to get my tongue pierced, she dared me that I wouldn't do it. The bet was if I did it, she would pay for it. I'm always up for a challenge and I said, "*Ok, let's go.*" We went into a piercing/ tattoo shop that we frequent and I got my tongue pierced. I sat through the process of this guy holding my tongue out in some clamps and putting a long needle through it, along with the bar and screwing the closure ball on top; it was complete.

    I told my bestie, "*Now pay the man.*" When my dad found out I had my tongue pierced, he questioned my sexuality. I didn't realize he thought I was testing the waters until one day we were watching Jerry Springer. I made a comment about a guy being gay. My dad asked, "*How do you know, is it because he has his tongue pierced?*"

I'VE GOT TO COMB MY HAIR

He asked in a quite annoyed tone. I busted out laughing. I said having your tongue pierced has nothing to do with your sexual orientation. My dad yelled out as I was leaving the living room, "*I don't know what the hell is going on with you and Annette, but you're hanging out in the village and you're turning into freaks.*" This really amused me. I think I secretly liked getting under my dad's skin. It was my payback; however, gay was certainly one thing I was not. The village is known for its heavy gay population, but it's also known for its eccentric-artsy influence.

My parents always seemed curious as to what type of person I was. My mother seemed to think that I was having sex when I was not and my father thought that I could possibly be gay because of my change in style. I was neither promiscuous nor gay.

I think in my mom's world, promiscuity for teen girls was the norm and she could not relate outside of that box. My grandmother use to always tell us what good girls did not do, and while I got a little adventurous, there were just some areas I would not cross. I did lose my virginity to my high school boyfriend around my senior year of school, but he was the only one I allowed to touch me.

    After graduation I knew I had to make a decision of what I was going to do with my life. So, after much thought, I decided to return to Florida with my grandmother in hopes to attend college with some of my peers. New York wasn't hard for me to leave as I was ready to get on with my life and put some things behind me. I knew I was going to miss my friends, but I also knew that it was time to go.

    My father and my stepmother had made arrangements for me to fly down to Miami to meet them; they were there in Ft. Lauderdale visiting my stepmother's parents. When I got off my flight my father realized that I had a tattoo on my arm. He didn't see it while we were in New York (wink). He gave me an entire lecture from Miami to Ft. Lauderdale about how I would not be able to give blood with that tattoo on my arm. My dad said, *"You're going to regret that one day."* Let's just say he turned out to be right. Smh!! I took the bus from Ft. Lauderdale into Tallahassee, FL.

This was the last time I rode greyhound. It was the worst experience ever because I had to sit next to a man who had this awful body odor and then I ended up sitting on a bus in front of a Mexican who decided he wanted to rub his fingers in my hair. I gave him a cursing that his distant relatives probably felt. He would have gotten cut too if he got out of control because I had my box cutter in my pocket waiting to slice him up.

I was now back at home with my grandmother, Madea. My grandmother was not ready to let me be the adult I thought I was at that time. She fell back into her natural sheltering ways; I felt smothered. I wasn't driving yet, nor did I have a car. This was an 18 year old's nightmare. I pushed myself to stay because I wanted to go to college along with some of my old friends from Chattahoochee; although it was hard for me to adjust being back in a small town and not being able to just go when I wanted to.

In addition, my grandmother wanted to know my every move and tried to control where

I'VE GOT TO COMB MY HAIR

I went and what I did. Some old friends picked me up and we drove forty-five minutes to Tallahassee, FL to register for school. Tallahassee has two major Universities, Florida State and Florida A&M. I of course wanted to attend Florida A&M as it was one of the most reputable Historically Black Colleges on the east coast.

All of my friends were going to community college first so I decided to do the same. This is where the nightmare continued. I took my placement test and stood in this long line to register for classes. My financial aid had not been approved as of yet. Since I had no documentation to prove I was a Florida resident, I was considered an out of state student.

I remember finally getting up to the front desk only to be told that I had to pay an astronomical amount for my classes. The lady who gave me my receipt must have noticed the pained look on my face after looking at the white paper with my tuition fees on it. She said in a very understanding tone, "*Be prepared to pay for your classes just in case your financial aid does not come through.*" I went back home to my grandmother's very worried that day.

A year had gone by since I graduated high school as I wanted to take some time off before starting college. My grandmother didn't understand college forms, tuition, financial aid, and etc… she could not help me. My financial aid kept getting declined because my parents supposedly made too much money. I called my dad in sheer panic.

I told my dad the amount I needed to pay for school and he said he didn't have it. I cried. I asked him what happened to my college fund in a shaky voice, with tears rolling down my cheeks. My dad reminded me that he had my younger brothers to take care of as well and that he could not afford to pay my tuition.

I was so hurt and devastated. I even had some friends to tease me about not being able to get into school. I felt stuck and not knowing what to do; I even thought that I should return to New York. My mind begins racing with so many thoughts. I knew I had to make a decision and I had to make one fast!

I'VE GOT TO COMB MY HAIR

When I graduated high school, I gave myself two options, either I was going to go to college or I was going into the Air Force. Since college was no longer on the table, Air Force it was. My grandmother was not too thrilled about my decision to go into the Air Force. She asked me about college and I told her the Air Force will pay for it. She even called my dad pleading for him to talk me out of it. My mind was made up; I was going into the Air Force.

A friend invited me to a church service one evening. It was a revival located at one of those small Pentecostal churches. I don't remember the speaker's name, but I remember what she spoke to me. She said you have made a big decision. Some members of your family do not want you to go, but they have to understand that you are not the same little girl you used to be. I knew my grandmother was the culprit. She feared many things and her granddaughter going into the military was one of them. When I asked my grandmother if she was the one the prophet spoke about, she denied it. I knew it was her, but she didn't want me to know that she was afraid.

I'VE GOT TO COMB MY HAIR

Before I went into the military, I met a young man and he and I began dating. My grandmother did not like him from day one, but I always felt she just did not want to share me. He was about 5'10 with bronzy skin, an eight pack stomach, and a beautiful smile. He attended and played football for Florida A&M and was also attending ROTC at Florida State University. I met him through a mutual friend and honestly, I didn't think much of him at first. I hadn't done much dating outside of my high school boyfriend.

One day, my childhood friend and I were visiting some of her friends in Tallahassee. After leaving the friends' apartment, I saw a note on the passenger side of the car. I was riding with one of my childhood friends so I thought it was quite strange for someone to put a note on a passenger side of a car, however it turned out the note was for me.

Earlier that evening, my friend asked me to go with her to this guy's apartment, which he happened to live on the floor above her friends' apartment. I was a little hesitant at first, but I eventually agreed. We knocked on the door and Ceric asked, "*Who is it*?" She told him her name and he responded by saying he was busy. She told him to stop playing and open the door; however, he again replied that he was busy. He must've heard me say let's go because he then peeked through the peep hole to see who my friend had with her.

He cracked the door open and asked, "*Who's with you*?" She responded, "*This is my friend Shawnte.*" He then opened the door to let us in. I felt a little awkward because before hearing or seeing me, he acted as if he did not want to be bothered.

We talked to him for a while and it was apparent that he had a clear attraction to me, but I ignored it up until I got the note on the car. The note requested that I call him after I got off from work the next day and it was signed, "Ceric".

Initially, I thought he was interested in my friend, but after the two of them cleared that up, I agreed to go out on a date with him. We clicked right away. We talked about the military, working out, and our future. He did not understand why I wanted to go into the military as an enlisted person. He was going to be a commissioned officer upon graduation from college; however, there was no changing my mind about going into the Air Force.

I was determined that I would not fail in life and this was my chance to secure my future. I didn't know if he and I would continue to date as I was set to leave for basic training soon.

In my mind, I will be surrounded by new young men so there was no need to get serious with him. He wanted us to continue with our relationship so with a little convincing I decided to keep the relationship going. Shortly thereafter, I was on my way to San Antonio, Texas for basic training.

I'VE GOT TO COMB MY HAIR

I'VE GOT TO COMB MY HAIR

I'VE GOT TO COMB MY HAIR

My childhood friend and I were going to basic training together on the buddy system. We had to travel from Chattahoochee to Tallahassee to the recruiter's office. My grandmother drove me that morning and she fussed all the way there because I stayed out late partying with my friends the night before. She said no young lady should be hanging out that late at night.

I told my grandmother, I have done everything she requested. I come in when she wants me to and try not to hang out too often with my friends. I explained to her that I was no longer a baby and I had a life too, and I wanted to spend some time with my friends prior to going into the military.

Ceric surprised me at the recruiter's office. He came to see me after finishing up his final exams. I was so excited to see him! My grandmother on the other hand was not as she cautiously watched us. Ceric was afraid to give me the goodbye kiss I requested because my grandmother was watching. I didn't mind taking the risk as I was on my way to basic

I'VE GOT TO COMB MY HAIR

training anyway and didn't worry too much concerning any repercussions from her; besides I only asked for a kiss on the cheek.

    We were transported by van to Jacksonville, FL to in-process at the Military Entrance Processing Station (MEPS). We flew out of Jacksonville's Airport to San Antonio, TX the next day. Ceric bought me some calling cards so that I could call him every time we had a layover. I would stop at every pay phone so that I could call him. Each time I would call, he would sing to me "*Shawnte's (technically Chante) got a man at home*" by Chante Moore. I had some of the folks that were traveling to basic training to listen as well; although I think I annoyed my friend. LOL!!

    We arrived at Lackland Air Force Base at 3 a.m. I was tired from the long trip and was hoping to get some rest. Well, I was in for a rude awakening because there was no such thing as rest in basic training.

    When we arrived, they had us to line up in an assembly line format waiting for our names to be called, so that they could direct us onto the appropriate bus that will take us

I'VE GOT TO COMB MY HAIR

into our squadron. Once entering the bus and taking my seat, I tried to prepare my mind for what was ahead of me. It was still dark outside, but the base had street lights everywhere.

All the buildings looked the same as everything was uniformed. It was a short ride before we arrived at the barracks. I saw men lined up with funny looking hats that appeared somewhat similar to a cowboy hat; these were our training instructors. They were waiting to greet us, so I thought. It was not quite the greeting I was expecting.

As soon as the bus opened, I heard what sounded like barking. It was actually the training instructors yelling at everyone who got off the bus. I was thinking, "What in the world is this?".

When I got off the bus, one of the training instructors noticed my belt was missing from a belt loop. He barked at me saying, "*WHAT IS WRONG WITH YOUR FREAKING BELT?*" I had never heard freaking used so much that I actually thought it was funny. I busted out laughing; boy did that get me into a world of trouble. They begin yelling a hole into my chest or at least that's what it felt like. I threw my hands up and said, "*Whoa calm down.*" The training instructor got close up in my face and asked me if I was trying to attack him. I looked at him with that 'are-you-kidding me-confused' look. I mean, surely this was a misunderstanding… so to keep from getting jumped by three men I put my hands down. Then one of the training instructors asked me in somewhat of a southern drawl, "*WHAT IS YOUR FREAKING TRAINING STATMENT!*" I replied, "*Trainee Mckinnon reports*" nonchalantly with one eyebrow raised. My recruiter drilled the importance of knowing my training statement before getting to basic training and he was so right. They called me a freaking genius and left me alone. Whew…close call!

It didn't take long for me to get my act together and get accustomed to the military training life. My calm demeanor helped me to survive basic training. It was rare that I ever got frazzled by the training instructors or the obstacle courses. I was pretty athletic so the physical training was not too hard for me. **The ups and downs of life prior to the**

military prepared me for the mental aspects of the training.

Some of the women in my flight (a term the Air Force used for your unit) would say, *"Mckinnon we never see you cry."* My response, *"Aww this is nothing, you haven't met my grandmother."* This would make the ladies laugh. I guess my grandmother's yelling wasn't too bad after all. She prepared me for the military unknowingly. **Life has a way of coming back around full circle. What I thought was just too much aggravation as a child actually prepared me for another level of challenges that life presented.**

I went through basic training with a fair amount of ease up until one day. The day came where I felt like giving up. We had to walk six miles to what was called the "confidence course". This was our final rounds of obstacle training and I had to pass this course in order to graduate. It was over ninety degrees in San Antonio, TX that day. We were dressed for battle wearing our battle dress uniforms, which we call BDU(s) for short and carried our knapsack as we were going to be camping out in the field.

I'VE GOT TO COMB MY HAIR

I had on my cavalier helmet and flack vest to protect my body from bullets. The gear, including the knapsack, was quite heavy and especially draining in the heat. After walking half of the way, the heat started getting to me. I felt as though I could not take another step. The sweat was stinging my face where the sun had burnt me. I thought to myself, "This is crazy and not worth it!" Keep in mind, I had not given my life to Christ at this point so cursing was second nature to me. I said, "*F___k this, I'm going home*"; however, I had a friend from my brother flight that came along to encourage me to continue on. I thought I wasn't going to make it, but with a little nudge from a friend I was able to continue on the journey.

The training instructors belted off phrases that were ingrained into our minds along the way. They would yell things like... "**survival of the fittest, only the strong will survive.**" **It taught me that if my mind could assess it then I could obtain it. Proverbs 24: 10 states, if you falter in a time of trouble, how small are your strengths! I just**

could not give up as failure was not an option.

I made it through basic training and graduated. I didn't have any family members that could make it to my graduation and the friend that came to basic training with me was sent back home due to injuries as a result of training, but I was still content and happy I made it through. **There will be times in your life that you will have to walk alone. It was during this time that I learned to embrace the journeys that were designed specifically for me to travel. In doing this, I learned you will have to go alone at times, but God will always be with you even when you are not with him.**

After leaving basic training, I was sent to Biloxi, Mississippi, where I spent six weeks in training to learn my job. My job was personnel, which is human resources in civilian terms. I was happy that I got into the field I wanted. I had a nice cush job in the military and preferred it that way. I mean I am a girly girl and the military wasn't going to change that.

I'VE GOT TO COMB MY HAIR

My first duty station was in Sacramento, California. It was my first time on the west coast. In basic training, they give you the opportunity to list the top five places you would like to be stationed. My first choice was California. I wanted to be as far away from home as possible without actually leaving the country (I wasn't quite ready to leave the country yet).

The list was called the dream sheet. It truly lives up to its name because you get to list at least five places that you dreamt of living. When I got my orders telling me I will be reporting to McClellan Air Force Base in California, I was beyond ecstatic!

Before reporting to my duty station, I went back home to see my grandmother and Ceric. I was ready to go, but I was not ready to leave my boyfriend. I realized once boarding my plane that I had fallen in love and wasn't looking forward to being apart from him.

Ceric and I traveled to see each other often. We talked every day- almost all day long. We were determined to stay together no matter how far apart we were. There were times

I'VE GOT TO COMB MY HAIR

I would travel to see him without telling my grandmother that I was in town because I didn't want it to be an argument about where I would be staying.

My grandmother did not approve of me staying with Ceric. He wasn't having me spending my whole vacation at my grandmother's especially when he paid for my plane tickets. My grandmother would find out I was home because I always bumped into someone I knew from the hometown I grew up in. I would ask them not to tell my grandmother they saw me, but of course they went against my wishes and told anyway. I would get calls from my grandmother letting me have it about coming to visit and not letting her know.

I understood where she was coming from and why she was upset, but I always felt this was what I had to do to keep the peace. My grandmother was not ready to let go of me as her baby girl and she felt Ceric was separating me from my family. That wasn't quite the reality, but once she had something in her mind, you can forget about changing it. She could be quite stubborn and a force to be reckoned with. So, I picked my battles carefully.

Although my boyfriend and I were miles away, I remained faithful to him. I would not give any other guy a chance; I had tunnel vision. I had suitors that tried to date me, but I wouldn't budge.

After a year and half in Sacramento, CA, I got reassigned to Dover Air Force Base in Delaware. I met an older Sergeant who took a liking to me. She was a medium built Black-Hispanic with fair skin and beautiful long hair. She was a beautiful lady.

She always tried to encourage me to expand my horizons and not be so tied to a guy, because I was still quite young. She told me I reminded her of herself when she was my age and if she could do it all over again, she would do it differently.

She had been married twice and divorced twice. Some of my male counterparts would make jokes about how they would love to get with her and asked me to hook them up every time they saw us hanging out together. She'd just laugh when I would tell her some young 'horny wet behind the ear boy was admiring her'.

I'VE GOT TO COMB MY HAIR

The Sergeant poured a lot of wisdom in me during this time. I knew what she was saying to me had some validity, but I only saw through my own pair of lenses. In my mind, things were fine the way they were. I thought to myself, *Ceric and I would surely make it, we'll be fine.*

I was coming up to the end of my career and I was slapped with orders to deploy to Saudi Arabia for three months. I was not quite happy about this, but I made sure to put my separation paperwork in prior to leaving for my deployment.

Ceric and I had been talking about whether or not I should re-enlist or separate from the military. By this time, Ceric was a commissioned officer in the Air Force. Enlisted and Officers were not allowed to fraternize, but he and I managed to keep our individual careers secret from our counterparts.

Since Ceric was now a pilot in the Air Force and my career was ending, we thought it would be best if I just separated; as our relationship was detrimental to his career and his career was seemingly more important than mine at the time, or at least that's how Ceric made it appear. I, however, was ready to come out, get married, and finish school.

Shortly after returning home from Saudi Arabia, I separated from the military and moved back to Florida with Ceric. Although I was happy about us starting a new chapter in our lives, I never felt comfortable living with him. I was always taught that you never live with a man that you are not married to, but against my better judgment, I did it anyway.

Ceric and I seemed to have a fairly simple plan. I was going to enroll in school and he would take care of all the bills while I was attending school. I told him that I also wanted to work and eventually move out and have my own place. Shortly after, I eventually started working and was preparing to go to school in the fall. He was in the process of having a home built so our apartment living was temporary. Ceric was really good at taking care of the bills and being responsible and I loved that about him, but our bliss as a couple was short lived.

I'VE GOT TO COMB MY HAIR

I had learned that Ceric had some issues that I was not comfortable with, such as pornography and chatting with various women through different internet sites. I knew about the pornography, but I did not know to what extent his interest was in them; that was until I started to notice he was getting new videos in the mail weekly.

I didn't make much of a fuss about it at first. Ceric's habits began to noticeably change. There was a time when I laid down for a nap or for the night, he would lay down with me. I would then wake up and find myself sleeping alone.

One night I walked out of the room to look for him, as soon as I entered the living room, he would slap his laptop close. When I would ask what he was doing, he would say. *"Oh I'm just surfing the web."* I knew something was up with him because he literally jumped off the sofa when he saw me.

Things came to a head when he started to get careless and leave his email and chats open. One particular day, I was on his laptop and a chat popped up. I looked at the chat and it said "hey baby". I was curious, so I responded back saying "hey". She then went on to ask how was his girlfriend doing amongst some other things; so to keep her from catching on that it was me and not Ceric, I ended the conversation quickly.

This really peaked my curiosity and I began to search Ceric's chat transcripts and I found different dialogues from numerous women. They say if you go looking, you might find what you're looking for. That saying was an understatement to say the least. My hands were shaking and my blood was boiling.

When Ceric got home from work I confronted him about the situation, but of course he got defensive and angry with me, asking me what was I doing looking through his things. I was so mad with him that I told him that he was sleeping on the couch that night. I locked him out the bedroom and went to the room and cried myself to sleep. I was so hurt by things I found in Ceric's computer and closet (Yes, I looked there too!) that I wanted vengeance!

I was working at a car dealership and there were a few guys there crushing on me. I started hanging out with one of the guys that took an interest in me. This is where the lies begin. I came home late one night and Ceric wanted to know where I had been. I told him I grabbed a bite to eat with one of the ladies I worked with, but that was furthest from the truth. I did grab a bite to eat, however, it was with the guy from work. I found myself in somewhat of an emotional affair. While I never slept with this guy, I began to hang out with him more often.

During this time, things between Ceric and I were growing colder and colder. One day while washing dishes, I calmly told Ceric that I was leaving him. I said, *"I'm not sure what you are looking for, but clearly you do not feel you have it here and I hope you find what you are looking for."* I was hoping Ceric would fight for the relationship and understand my pain, but instead he continued to look at the TV and did not respond to me. He had chiseled features and his jaws begin to tighten so I knew I had gotten under his skin; however, tight jaws were not what I was looking for. I was looking for communication.

Ceric was a bit controlling so I knew my staying out late would push his buttons. I hung out all night with my guy friend and did not return home until six in the morning. Ceric is nocturnal so he is usually up all night and I'm normally home before he goes to bed. Well, this time when I got home, he was already in the bed and I knew it was going to be trouble.

    I turned on the light in the room, hoping he was sleeping, but he was wide awake. He snapped at me telling me to, "*Turn the f-ing light off!*" I switched the light off quickly as I knew this could turn ugly real fast. I tiptoed to the bathroom to get in the shower. Once I was in the shower, I could feel danger. I couldn't make sense of things, but I knew that it was time to go; things had gotten really bad.

    I cried out to God asking him to help me get out of the situation. I told God that I had become someone I was not and I wanted my life back. I asked him to protect me and not let Ceric harm me. Ceric had started showing signs of aggression so I wanted to be careful with him.

    A couple of days later, I got up early and left the house. I felt really liberated that day because I decided that I was leaving

I'VE GOT TO COMB MY HAIR

Ceric and moving out. I did not tell him that I was moving out that day and I figured I didn't have to. I went to Captain D's and ordered fried catfish, French fries and sweet tea. Ceric didn't like for me to eat fried foods as he was a health freak. He controlled me and I was too naïve to realize it. When I got home with my forbidden food, I begin to pull out the boxes that we were saving to use to move out into the new house.

Ceric was up in the other room doing pushups. He had been sleeping in the other room, because I kept him locked out of our room. I went in the room to ask him for the packing tape and between clenched teeth he told me to get out of the room. I noticed that Ceric had taken my flight suit and teddy bears he bought me out of my room. I loved teddy bears and Ceric always bought them for me. He called himself taking them from me. I was actually shocked, but I shrugged my shoulders and walked out of the room.

Ceric eventually came out of the room and was not thrilled about seeing me pack. Things went south fairly quickly as Ceric came out of the room cursing, telling me I need to get my

I'VE GOT TO COMB MY HAIR

S__T (You know, sugar honey ice tea) out of the way. He threw my food in the garbage and my tea down the drain. He started throwing the boxes and pulling my clothes out the drawer all while yelling at me telling me to get out. He threw the dining room table over and dishes came crashing to the floor.

I had enough of his tirade and so I started cursing him back. I told him to leave me alone and go play with his internet chicks in his room. This ticked him off; Ceric came charging at me with anger in his eyes! I happened to have scissors in my hand because I was cutting tape to pack up my boxes.

When he started coming my way, I snapped the scissors open and told him to bring it! I told Ceric that I would slice him up. I yelled, "*I wish you would, I will f__k you up.*" Ceric stopped dead in his tracks. I guess he knew I meant what I was saying. I was really shook up by his behavior. I dialed 911 because he was tearing the apartment up.

My nerves were so bad that I accidentally dropped the phone and the call dropped. The 911 dispatcher called back and Ceric grabbed the phone before I could and told the 911 dispatcher that his girlfriend was belligerent and tried to cut him. I could not believe my ears. Ceric had turned the tables on me. Two police officers came to the house and I was totally distraught by the current events.

    The policemen soon separated us and got our individual stories of what took place. The officer that spoke to my boyfriend came over to me saying that Ceric told him that I tried to cut him and that he has a cut between his forefinger and thumb. I was unsure how Ceric got the cut because I did not touch him with the scissors. I explained to the police officer that I wasn't sure how Ceric got the cut.

    He did eventually get the scissors from me by twisting my arm behind my back, but I only threatened him to protect myself. The police officers asked him to leave the apartment for the night and that either one of us could file an injunction against the other. I told the officer that wouldn't be necessary as I was packing to leave anyway.

    I was really hurt and disappointed that Ceric would lie on me to the police. I thought I was going to be arrested. I asked him why would he lie on me, as he gathered a few clothes to leave for the night. The police stayed until he left. I had never seen Ceric so enraged before and I was worried that he was going to come back home in the middle of the night. I barricaded the front door with furniture and locked myself in the bedroom. I called Ceric's mom to let her know what had taken place that day. She said she was going to call him, but I begged her not to say anything to him until I moved out. I didn't know how Ceric would react if he knew I told his mother what took place.

    The next morning Ceric came home; I heard him pushing the furniture back from the door. He was a pretty strong guy. I was very silent in the room and I didn't come out. He came in to shower and get ready for work; I also went to work. While I was at work, a police officer came looking for me to serve me injunction paperwork.

    I couldn't believe that Ceric got a restraining order against me! I guess he was afraid that I was going to file one against him; therefore he took action first. He told me that I could not go back to the apartment without a police escort. I had never in all my years dealt with such a humiliating situation like this before. I was pissed and deeply hurt that Ceric would take me through so much. I had some money in the bank so I checked myself into a hotel for the night and I called my guy friend from work to tell him about the restraining order.

Ceric, in my mind, had stooped to an all-time low. I went to the police station the next morning to get an escort so that I could gather a few of my belongings. I felt like I was being treated as a criminal, but my only crime was trying to leave a relationship that was no longer working. I was so mad at Ceric and really wanted revenge.

I walked in the apartment as the police officer stood by the door and emptied the apartment of every pot, pan, and utensil. I looked at Ceric and begin to cry. I asked him how could he do such a thing to me. It was like a lump had formed in my throat and between the gulp and tears I yelled, "*I HATE YOU*!!" Ceric was on the phone with his mother at the time.

I'VE GOT TO COMB MY HAIR

I heard him tell his mother, "*She said she hate me.*" He was acting macho and unfazed by the humiliation and pain he was putting me through. I could not understand how someone, one who claimed to love me and treated me so well throughout the years, could be so vindictive in a split second. Our relationship came to a nasty end.

I decided that I would return home to my grandmother's. My car was loaded with all the belongings I could fit in my car and traveled back to Chattahoochee, which was an hour and a half from where Ceric and I lived. I didn't know what I would say to my grandmother, but I wasn't ready to say much to her. Although I was certain she would be happy to have me back home. I got to my grandmother's house and pulled into the driveway, dreading the impending conversation I would have to have with her.

I knocked on the door and opened it with my key. I yelled, "*Madea it's Shawnte.*" She said, *"Hi baby."* I then told her I would be staying with her for a while. Madea was in her room in the bed and she didn't ask any questions; she just said, "*Alright*" in her normal, soft tone. She then told me to take my things to the guest room.

The next morning Madea and Granddad were outside sitting under the car porch. She called for me to come outside saying her and granddad would like to speak to me. My grandmother shared with me that she called to speak to me a couple of days ago, but Ceric told her I was not there and he thought that I was with her. She said that he also told her that I tried to cut him. Before I could catch myself, I said "*He is a lying Negro.*"

I think my grandmother was shocked by my verbiage as she has never heard me speak in that manner in front her, but it also tickled her slightly. I recounted the events to my grandparents and after telling them what took place, my grandmother said, "*I believe you, you have no reason to lie to us.*"

My grandfather looked off as if he was in deep thought then he turned a looked at me and said, "*Baby, you never try to leave in front of a man.*" I said, "*Now you tell me granddad, I wish someone would have told me prior to all of this.*" Granddad then said, "*Well I'm not going to have no foolishness around here because I will put bullets in him.*" Granddad was always our protector and even though I was an adult, he was still willing to protect me.

I appreciated my grandparents support because there was a rough emotional road ahead of me and I needed all the support I could get. The next day I was awakened by the ringing of the phone. There was a phone in my room on the nightstand by the bed. I answered the phone and it was one of my grandmother's prayer partners. In a sweet, sympathetic voice, my grandmother's prayer partner said, "*We are praying for you honey and everything is going to be alright.*"

I was livid and grateful at the same time. I asked my grandmother to please not share my personal business with others. It was an already sensitive issue for me. My grandmother responded, "*You better be glad people are praying for you honey.*" She had a point, but I was still mad.

Ceric and I had a court date to address the injunction. I had to travel to the area where Ceric and I lived to attend court. I didn't know what to expect, but I wanted the madness to stop. About a week before I had to

I'VE GOT TO COMB MY HAIR

attend court with Ceric, my grandmother received a call and I answered the phone. It was a man asking to speak to Evangelist Gainer.

My grandmother was sitting in the den watching TV so I just took the phone to her and sat down in the den to watch TV along with her. I heard her tell the man on the phone that I was her granddaughter. She then pulled the phone from her ear and advised me that the gentleman on the phone was Prophet Ron and asked if I would like to speak to him.

Prophet Ron had asked her to speak to me. I told my grandmother no because I was afraid of what he would say to me. She told me, *"Girl you better get this phone."* When Madea speaks, you just listen. I took the phone from my grandmother and reluctantly said hello.

I began walking with the phone back to my room as I didn't know what the man was going to say to me. Prophet Ron said hello back and started to speak into my life. He told me, *"There is a young man that is tugging at your heart, but he is not the one God has ordained for you."* This man had never seen me before, but he went on to tell me that I was an attractive young lady and men were like caterpillars always trying to creep up and get me.

He said with much conviction, "*God wants all of you and not some of you.*" Prophet Ron also told me that I was smart and that he saw me working with money. We ended the call, but not before inviting me to church. He said he would be in Florida doing a revival and he would like for me to attend. I learned later that Prophet Ron lived in Georgia.

When Prophet Ron came into town for the revival, my grandmother and I attended. It was a little petite old church with very few members. He asked if I was the young lady he spoke to over the phone and I told him yes. He asked me to come up because he wanted to pray for me. When I got to the front, he said, "*The young man has told a lie on you and now you have to go to court.*"

I was shocked by how dead on he was! He further stated, "*God has been dealing with you about him and he is not who he says he is.*" I nodded as I knew what he was talking about. He prayed for me and instructed me to turn my plate down for four days. He said no foods;

just liquids for four days and watch God turn the case around.

I did as Prophet Ron instructed me to do; however, I struggled with what he said because I still loved Ceric very much in spite of what he was putting me through. I went into the bathroom praying for God to turn it around and make Ceric into the man he needed to be for me.

I call this my Hezekiah moment. I tried turning my face to the wall, hoping to get the Prophet to give me a different word. It didn't quite work out that way for me. Prophet Ron had told me so many people were praying for me at the time; God just stepped in and pulled me up out of the situation. I was torn between logic and my feelings and while I knew deep down Prophet Ron was right, I so wanted him to be wrong.

The court date came and I was expecting a turnaround just as Prophet Ron said it will be. Ceric got there just in time for our hearing. They escorted us into the judge's chambers and I did not expect what came next.

The judge read the police report and laid into me like nobody's business. I was in utter shock. I explained to the judge that I was only acting in self-defense when I threatened Ceric, but I never cut him. The judge told me to be quiet. He said I've seen women smaller than you whip men bigger than him. I looked at Ceric and said, "*Are you not going to tell the truth?*"

Ceric would not look at me; I begin to think it was some kind of conspiracy going on. Ceric's father was a judge and I thought clearly there were some strings pulled here on Ceric's behalf. The judge did agree to drop the charges and let me get the rest of my things out the apartment. I was in tears. Once again Ceric had managed to humiliate me. I was too naïve to see that God turned it around for me. He did it in such a way that I would not have anything on my record. **I had built my own blueprint of how things were supposed to go once the prophecy was given.** I was disappointed that Ceric didn't get the slap on the hand I thought he was going to get.

I drove back to Chattahoochee praying and talking to God. I wanted to give my life to Christ, but I wasn't quite ready for the commitment. I really needed God, if I never

I'VE GOT TO COMB MY HAIR

felt I needed him before. I was in the bed, but I was awake feeling extremely exhausted and in emotional pain so much so that my body ached.

At the age of 24, I found myself back in the house with my grandparents, the home I grew up in. It was hard to conceptualize the major turn my life took. I felt stuck, like I was suffocating and losing ground.

I thought Ceric was the love of my life… and to make matters worse, I was the talk of the family. Some were happy that I was hurting as it avenged them of me being successful. I didn't realize what some folks thought of me until I was down. Some of them said very hurtful and mean things to me.

I even had one family member say to me, "*See, you're not so perfect.*" I began to wonder why was everyone kicking me while I was down, but I guess the only way for anyone to kick me is I had to be down already. I simply lived my life not really bothering anyone, but I learned my life bothered others.

While I was lying in bed one afternoon, I overheard my grandfather speaking to my grandmother about me. "*Essie has the baby come out the room*", granddad asked Madea. My grandfather has called me the baby since I was a little girl. "*No, Thready she will come out when she's ready*", my grandmother responded. I was sleeping all the time. I just wanted to sleep my life away. Being awake and conscious would force me to deal with reality and I just didn't have the strength to deal with my truth at the time. I later learned I was going through what is called the exhaustion stage of depression, which is the third phase.

After hearing my grandfather's concern for me, I decided to come out of the room to at least show my face. "*Hi Granddad*", I said. He looked at me with a concerned look on his face. He said, "**Baby, are you going to comb your hair**?" I just looked at him and said, "**Yes Granddad, I'm going to comb my hair.**" I guess my grandfather thought, wow, this girl looks a hot mess! I had a short haircut, and my hair was sticking straight up like a porcupine.

I went back into the room, got in the bed and drifted off to sleep. My hair was the least of my concerns. The next morning I got up and went into the bathroom. I looked at my hair and thought to myself, **MAN, I've got to comb my hair.** This was a pivotal moment for me. I looked in the mirror and told myself, *Shawnte you are not going out like this!* So, I begin to comb my hair with tears running down my face. That's when life began again for me and I started picking up the pieces, putting my life back together.

I'VE GOT TO COMB MY HAIR

TRANSITIONS

I started a new job and after living with my grandparents for five months, I moved to Tallahassee, FL in my own apartment. I was fresh out of the military so I was still trying to adjust to civilian life. In addition, I was adjusting to my life without Ceric. Ceric and I both struggled with being apart. There was a push and pull between the two of us. I knew in my heart he was not for me and we were not healthy for each other. I wanted my life to be so much different from the relationships I saw growing up.

I witnessed some very tumultuous relationships growing up. I vowed never to have a relationship like the ones I had been exposed to. **Sometimes the very things that we are running from are the very things that we run into when we are not healed and delivered.** I needed to be healed from my past, but I didn't know how to really do it. I took matters into my own hands, thinking I knew the answers.

Thoughts of Ceric haunted me night and day. I woke up thinking about him; I went to sleep thinking about him. I even tried dating a little, but nothing would stop his name from ringing in my heart. Ceric would call me from time to time as I would him. We even met up and went out to dinner a few times, but just as old friends reminiscing. We talked about all the places we traveled together and the restaurants we frequented.

 I let Ceric in because I felt I needed his comfort. When Ceric learned I was dating, he made it clear to me that no other man would come before him. He even threatened me saying if he could not have me no one else can! I told him that I would report him to his commander. He apologized to me and we ended the conversation.

 I knew Ceric was dating as well, but he tried to keep that hidden from me. Although Ceric had shown signs of aggression in the past, I kept telling myself that Ceric would not hurt me. I went through a period where I had a few guys calling me at the same time; one from my past, including Ceric, as I was never one to entertain multiple men.

 I could literally count on one hand the number of men I've been serious with. Some were men attempting to pursue me. The most they got out of me was a phone conversation. It just seemed like so many were pulling at me all at one time. I got so sick of them that I changed my phone number. I thought surely this would resolve the issue in my young mind.

Ceric and I were speaking to each other less and less. I didn't feel the need to give him my new number. Ceric obviously did not take too well of me changing my number that he decided to show up at my apartment at one in the morning.

I had no idea who was ringing my doorbell at this time of night. It kind of alarmed me so I didn't respond at first, but the ringing would not stop. I finally got up the nerve to ask who it was at the door. That's when Ceric let me know it was him.

I was shocked that he was at my door. He and I had been broken up for at least a year or so by now and it just didn't make sense. He was not happy that it took me so long to open the door. He immediately asked, *"What the f__k took you so long to answer the door."* I asked him where he was coming from. He told me he came from home, which is a two hour drive from where I lived. I asked him what he was doing in Tallahassee. He told me that he called me and could not reach me so he was worried. I looked at his eyes and could tell he was enraged. I heard this still voice in my ear say, "**Be calm**." Something was telling me to be calm.

    Ceric walked into my apartment and proceeded to my bedroom. I guess he was looking to see if someone was in the room. While he was in there, he picked up my cell phone and dialed his number. He came out of my room and asked me why I changed my number and told me not to do that again. I didn't object or argue because the voice kept telling me to stay calm.

    Ceric ended up staying the night without touching me. I prayed and asked God, not to let him harm me or touch me. **God, yet again answered my prayer in my naiveté.** Ceric went home the next morning and everything was peaceful. Although Ceric's behavior was toxic, I was too bound to see it. I thought by pushing him away romantically I was doing fine, but the grip of our relationship continued to torment me.

I'VE GOT TO COMB MY HAIR

I didn't really tell anyone how I was tormented every day about him. It was my little secret. I just kept telling myself I will get through this. I was clubbing, drinking, and got involved with another guy, but none of those things healed my pain.

One of the supervisors at my job invited me to church for the family and friends Sunday service and I decided that I would go. I was really blessed by the service. I started attending more frequently. I was so amazed to see so many of my peers sold out for God and I mean sold out for real for real. I grew up in the church and was in the church most of my life, but church was not in me; however, there was something different transpiring on the inside of me.

I wanted what they had. I wanted to serve God and not be ashamed. It no longer looked like the Old person's religion. It was just so much freedom in this church! This church really tugged at my heart like no other had done in my past.

I was going through so many different things during this time. I had issues with management at my current job so I started looking for other jobs. I applied for a job at Florida State University as a Program Assistant; however, the director of the office thought that position was too mediocre for me and offered me a job that I did not apply for or consider.

    She called and advised me that they had a Senior Accountant position available that she thought was better suited for me. She asked me to apply for it; although I was a little nervous about it, I applied anyway. I ended up getting the job. When I got the job, my mind went back to what Prophet Ron had spoken to me a couple of years prior. He said he saw me working with money and I was good with numbers. His word came to pass!

    I was amazed by God and His promises. It was like God knew before I did that my heart was changing. One Sunday, I took what felt like a long walk down the aisle to rededicate my life to the Lord. When I got to the altar I was emotionally, physically, and spiritually exhausted.

    I was tired of doing things my own way. I remember telling God with slump shoulders that if you want me, here I am, but I need you to do something about this pain. My life transitioned that day! I started inviting others to church as well. I lost some friends along the way because they could not get with the new me, but I was ok with that. I went hard in the world so I was going hard for Christ and there was no stopping me.

I had some stumbles in the beginning, but I was not going back to the way things used to be. My Pastor taught us truth and not religion. He was compassionate about God's people and he had a way of making everyone feel loved and a part. He was my spiritual father.

I was trained to be a military soldier in the United States Armed Forces, but he taught me how to be a soldier in the Kingdom of God. I witnessed every chance I got. I even held bible study in my apartment. God was doing something new in me while being tormented by my past with Ceric became less and less.

I was growing spiritually, but this did not come without a great amount of warfare. This is when God birth out the prayer warrior in me. I always knew how to pray as my grandmother taught me this as a little girl, but God taught me how to war in prayer. I had family and friends come up against me like never before. It was painful, but it kept me on my knees and in my bible.

When the enemy wants to hurt you, he will use people. When God wants to bless you, he will use people. It's important that your armor is on so you can decipher the difference. I would go to God and ask why, but I learned He allowed these things to get me ready for what was ahead.

In 2007, I woke up and sat straight up in the middle of my bed. I felt in my spirit that I would be moving. I felt the urge so strongly that when I got to my office at Florida State University, I called my mom who resides in New York to tell her I was moving. She asked me, *"Where are you moving to?"* I was on my office computer at the time perusing Black Enterprise Website and happened to come across an article that talked about the top 10 places young black professionals are thriving in.

I said, *"Ummm"*…. as I was going down the list, then without much thought, I blurted out *"Charlotte, NC."* Neither I nor my mom knew anything about Charlotte, but I knew it was where I was going. My mom connected me with a cousin who was living in Charlotte at the time.

After connecting with my cousin, I made plans to visit this unknown area that I felt God leading me to. My first trip to Charlotte was great, but I didn't get to see much of it before it was time for me to head back to Tallahassee. It didn't matter much that I didn't see all of Charlotte; I knew God wanted me there so I went home to prepare for the move.

When I got back to Tallahassee I started applying for jobs. I applied for at least 20 jobs a day. I applied everywhere. I stayed in prayer asking God to guide me and give me direction concerning the move. Meanwhile, God was tugging on my heart to join a particular auxiliary at church. I didn't understand why God wanted me to join this auxiliary as I was preparing to move. I would soon find out why I needed to join.

One day the strangest thing happened to me. I got an ingrown toenail on my big toe and it was swollen. I've never had an issue with my toes before, so I blamed it on my cousin's friend sneakers I borrowed while visiting Charlotte. I was thinking this is what I get for wearing other people's shoes. I tried to ignore the growing problem on my toe, but it got infected and I couldn't ignore it any longer.

    I made an appointment with a podiatrist so I could get my toe checked out. Once I got into the doctor's office, I was so nervous and talking a mile a minute to the nurse. I told her I had done my research online and it said my toe will have to be cut to remove the ingrown nail and infection. While I was expressing my concerns, the nurse smiled and assured me that I would be fine. She then put her hand on my chair and closed her eyes as if she was praying.

    I asked her if she was praying for me. I said, "*Please pray because I'm scared.*" She looked at me again with a smile and told me I would be fine. What she said next caught me off guard. She began speaking to me about the move I was preparing for. I did not know this lady at all and it was my first time seeing her. I then realized she was a prophetess.

I'VE GOT TO COMB MY HAIR

She said, "*You are supposed to be moving.*" I nodded yes. She said, "**God said he's been doing everything you ask so why are you wavering now.**" I looked at her trying to fight back my tears. I really don't like crying and I didn't want to cry in the public.

Doubt had crept in on me and I kept asking God if I was really supposed to move. She went on to tell me about my gift. She said, "*You have a gift like mine, but you won't use it. You will say if they don't have it by now they will never get it.*"

I was notorious for this line and I would say it more often than not. I laughed a little because I knew she was telling the truth. She said, "*You must speak because there are people around you that need to hear you speak.*" She told me many things during that appointment, but she did not allow me to leave before telling me I need to do what God is telling me to do. She further stated, "*There is something you are supposed to be doing but you have not done it yet, God said do it.*" I knew she was talking about the auxiliary at church.

I was in awe with God after leaving the doctor's office that day. The bible tells us in 1 Corinthians 1:26-28, **For consider your calling, brethren, that there were not many wise according to the flesh, not many mighty, not many noble; but God has chosen the foolish things of the world to shame the wise, and God has chosen the weak things of the world to shame the things which are strong, and the base things of the world and the despised God has chosen, the things that are not, so that He may nullify the things that are,...** God used an ingrown toenail to get a very important message to me and this woman of God had the word in her mouth.

    I was still hoping I had missed the call to join this auxiliary at church, but they called for it the following Sunday. They made an announcement that they were calling for new altar call workers to join the team. I knew I had to be obedient and join; therefore I made sure I was at the next meeting at church.

    During the meeting, my pastor said something so profound. He said, "*This is exactly where I started.*" He told us he was on a prayer team before going into his calling to preach. He continued to say that this was just the beginning for us. In my mind, I said no, not that preaching thing again.

Many times I received prophecies that I would preach. I was seven years old when a prophet called me out and told me that I would preach. I just thought it would be one of those prophecies that never came to pass. LOL!! Nonetheless, I begin working in the ministry and God blessed me tremendously.

When I went back to my follow up appointment at the podiatrist, the same nurse was there that spoke to me before. She looked at me and said, *"You look good and you did what God told you to do."* I nodded yes. She began to tell me how God was going to open the door I had been praying for.

She said, *"It's coming fast so be prepared and it will happen in the next few months."* She spoke more into my life that day. … I thanked her and asked for her phone number just in case I needed to call her in the future. She said I will give you my number, but you will not need it. My heart was just overjoyed by God's love for me that he did not let me miss His word.

I'VE GOT TO COMB MY HAIR

    I began to prepare myself for the move as instructed. I was all set to go. I patiently and not so patiently waited for my open door, but in my heart, I knew God was going to move. In my obedience, God opened the door just as she said. The job opened up just in time for me to close on my brand new house.

    During one of my visits to Charlotte, God impressed upon me to put a contract on a new home. I felt a little crazy afterwards, but I was so sure when I did it. **It was like God placed His hand on my back and said it's ok, you can do it.** I wanted to spend my last Sunday in Tallahassee in my home church.

    My pastor knew that I was moving. He had one of the Elders to tell me that he wanted to pray for me before I left. I was a little nervous about the move, but I had my game face on. After my pastor prayed for me, he told me to calm all my fears and all my worries, this move was ordained by God. I was just so amazed at how God strategically set me up for this move. **1 Samuel 15:22,** *But Samuel replied: "Does the LORD delight in burnt offerings and sacrifices as much as in obeying the LORD? To* *obey is better than sacrifice, and to heed is better than the fat of rams.*

I'VE GOT TO COMB MY HAIR

I'VE GOT TO COMB MY HAIR

THE STRUGGLE

I was excited to start my new chapter in Charlotte. God had spoken so many promises to me through His servants and I just could not wait to see the manifestation of His word; however, I still had a little bit of fear of the unknown. I settled in my brand new house. As I stood in my kitchen, I begin reminiscing about the day I was standing in the kitchen of the model home telling God that I wanted this particular model.

God truly answered my prayers just as the nurse told me He would. There was much I needed to learn about the place God sent me and why, but I was ready to receive my land of milk and honey. Unfortunately, my new territory did not come without a new set of struggles.

The job that God opened for me was trouble from the start. I just knew I was going to walk in and excel as I had done in prior jobs. Boy was I wrong about that. I realized fairly quickly that I was not liked, but I could not put my finger on why. I thought to myself, why God would open a door for me to work with such difficult people.

Right before I left Florida, my pastor told me I would speak on great platforms. I just worked as an altar call worker in his church. I knew what he was referring to, but I tried my best to deny it. I even asked one of my girlfriends what was Rev talking about. She said, "*Girl you know what Rev is talking about.*"

The day finally came where I had to face what Rev was speaking of. My new pastor approached me on a Sunday at church to ask me about my call to ministry. I tried to talk my way out of it by saying I mean I could be called to usher.

He dismissed my obvious reluctance to acknowledge a call to preach. He said I want you to come to a meeting tomorrow night at 7 o'clock. I agreed, but I didn't know I was walking into a minister's training meeting. When I got to the meeting, I knew the time had come for me to stop running from the thing that was spoken over my life at the young tender age of seven.

I'VE GOT TO COMB MY HAIR

    I finally accepted my call to preach. Once I accepted my call, doors begin to open. I spoke on radio shows, in conferences, and at my church. **It was almost as if I had been thrust into something that had been waiting on me my whole life.** With my acceptance of ministry came a greater level of warfare.

    After being on my job for several years, the time had come for me to resign. Management was working diligently to get me terminated. God had covered me over the years from all the traps that were set for me on the job, but the time had come for me to move on and I was ready. Shortly thereafter, I experienced death of a loved one, business deals fell through, financial crisis, health issues, heartbreak, betrayal and disappointments. It was one setback after another.

    I kept my momentum for a while. I woke up believing tomorrow was going to be a better day. I pushed in prayer and studied continuously. People looked on in pity not knowing what to say. Loved ones could not hide their concerns for me. I can hear their thoughts, wondering if I would make it out. Honestly, some days I myself did not know how

I was going to make it or if "out" was an option for me.

My strength seemed to wane and I found myself saying God, if you don't hold me up, I will not make it. There were some mornings where I would wake up with tears in my eyes. I wanted to scream my pain to the world, but instead I held my face like a flint and declared all is well. The story of the Shunammite woman left quite an impression on me (**2 Kings 4:8-37**).

In spite of having a dead son at home, she declared all was well on her journey to find the prophet who prophesied that God will give her a son. Now the prophesied son was dead. She had so much faith that even death could not shake her and you know what? God breathed life into her dead son.

God kept me surrounded by godly soldiers that would always speak life and pray for me when I felt down. **Your struggle will teach you there is much more life after death.** My grandmother who raised me passed away. She had been battling cancer for some time before God called her home. One of the last things she said to me was, "*I know one thing you all are* *going to be alright.*" I knew God had reassured my grandmother that she could go home with Him because He was going to ensure that her family would be taken care of. Her words also reassured me that everything was going to be fine.

    I was no longer working a regular 9 to 5 and begin pushing my dreams and ministry. A couple of months before leaving my job, I launched a radio show. God placed it on my heart to create a show to minister to His people. My grandmother got a chance to hear the show before she died. She was very proud and told me to keep talking. I laughed when she told me that because for years people told me I needed to be quiet. **My mouth is my weapon against the enemy. He worked hard attempting to steal my voice, but God told me to speak so I spoke.**

    The warfare in my life grew more intense. I got an offer to work on a new upcoming TV/radio show ministry. I was really excited about the opportunity and was looking forward to continuing ministry. The guys presented a good pitch to me, but it turned out to be a botch deal. One of the guys was only interested in getting to know me.

I later learned that this guy was hoping for a relationship with me and used the show as a form of connection. In addition, it was revealed by two prophets that the guy was praying against my future husband and marriage. I felt really betrayed and disgusted!

My money was running out and I really needed my businesses to take off. As if the money issues were not enough, I got hit with a major blow. I was diagnosed with Multiple Sclerosis. I looked the doctor in the face with a blank stare and she got up to give me a hug. She said I know I just gave you hard information.

I could not believe what I was hearing. I went to God and asked why. Why did I have to leave my job security, lose my grandmother, and my health all around the same time? God reminded me of everything he had brought me through. This time, hindsight was 20/20:

- ➢ He reminded me that death came knocking at my door when I lived with my ex.

- ➢ He reminded me that death came to my finances when my bank accounts were blacked out years ago.
- ➢ He reminded me death came to my heart when I was separated from my parents.
- ➢ He reminded me death came to my health when I thought I was going to lose my mind.
- ➢ He reminded me that through it all He kept me and gave me much more life after death.

He taught me that through him I am made strong. So, during the mornings that MS would attack my body, and I found myself down on the floor, I would plead the blood of Jesus. I know the blood never loses its power. I would cry out to God when I could not move until the attacks would release my muscles.

God showed me that though the attacks may come, it is His power that protects. He is Jehovah Nissi, the banner of protection. **But in that coming day no weapon turned against you will succeed. You will silence every voice raised up to accuse you. These benefits are enjoyed by the servants of the Lord; their**

vindication will come from me. I, the L<small>ORD</small>**, have spoken! (Isaiah 54:17, NLT)**

It is through your struggles that tenacity and endurance is built. I learned that God never does anything in the public that He has not prepared you for in the private. The warfare was just an indicator of the much more I have to live. 1 Peter 4:12-14(NLT) states, **Dear friends, don't be surprised at the fiery trials you are going through, as if something strange were happening to you.** [13] **Instead, be very glad—for these trials make you partners with Christ in his suffering, so that you will have the wonderful joy of seeing his glory when it is revealed to all the world.**

So, you know what I do now… I just look in the mirror and continue to comb my hair. **Psalms 119:71- It is good for me that I was afflicted, That I may learn Your statutes.**

I'VE GOT TO COMB MY HAIR

I'VE GOT TO COMB MY HAIR

LIFE LESSONS

There are times in life when we are hit with unexpected curve balls. When these things hit, we question the necessity of the trial. It can be very difficult to understand how our trials are an important part of our destiny.

As a child, I could not understand why I had to be separated from my parents. There is a song I love by Twinkie Clark and Reverend Richard White Clean entitled, *"Accept What God Allows"*. This concept took a long time for me to understand considering he was allowing me to endure pain, and in some cases, extreme pain.

In Romans 8:18 it states, yet what we suffer now is nothing compared to the glory he will reveal to us later (NLT). My grandmother had what I needed to carry out my God given assignment and that is to preach/teach the Gospel. My parents were carriers of the DNA I needed.

God has restored my mom and she is now a Christian working in ministry (Won't he do it!!); neither she nor my father was submitted to God at the time I was born. My mother is a fighter and a woman of great strength and my father is a communicator, giver and very analytical. They passed these wonderful traits to me (Thank God!).

My grandmother carried out the assignment that was ordained by God to show me the ways of the Lord. You have to understand that God knows who you are and he will allow what is necessary for your purpose to be established. God says **"I knew you before I formed you in your mother's womb. Before you were born I set you apart and appointed you as my prophet to the nations. (Jeremiah 1:5, NLT)"**

My grandmother was assigned to a task that was no small feat. Can you imagine the attacks that came her way due to the assignment? Well, I can tell you she had many, but it was as if she knew she had something precious in her hands and she did her best to protect it. I got rerouted, at the time it appeared I was at a disadvantage.

God knew the gifting's He had placed in me so He allowed some folks to be rerouted to protect the assignment. **After the wise men were gone, an angel of the Lord appeared to**

I'VE GOT TO COMB MY HAIR

Joseph in a dream. **"Get up! Flee to Egypt (wilderness) with the child and his mother,"** the angel said. **"Stay there until I tell you to return, because Herod is going to search for the child to kill him (Matthew 2:13)."** The wilderness is your protection.

After returning to New York, God showed me that He will answer your prayers and the funny thing is when He does it, you may not like the results. God obviously knew I would return home, but I did not go until the appointed time. He returned me to New York when I was old enough to handle the situation. In addition, I was also ready to learn my next step lessons (I did this unknowingly). **Life is a training ground; always preparing you for your next steps (Destiny is calling you).**

When I'm asked about my upbringing, I often tell people that too much of my grandmother and too much of my parents would have been too bad for me. God knew exactly when to insert the change so that I would have a balance of both extremes.

The bible tells us in **1 Thessalonians 5:16-18** to **"Always be joyful. Never stop praying. Be thankful in all circumstances, for**

this is God's will for you who belong to Christ Jesus." It is God's will that we stay in connection with Him. We probably wouldn't connect with God if there was no trouble. It is our prayers that keep us connected.

In addition, I learned to love myself and that I had value. My relationship with my ex-boyfriend taught me the importance of valuing who I am and what I have to offer. The enemy knows who you are long before you do. He doesn't wait until you are an adult to devise a plan of attack. He usually comes before you can recognize who you are. **He plants seeds of doubt, worthlessness, and fear as early as he can in hopes it will blossom into a bush of bitterness, hate, and defeat.**

These things usually spill over into our adulthood. When you are not delivered, you are toxic to yourself and those around you. Additionally, you link up with people who match what's going on inside of you. **You attract what's in you.** This, my friend, is what the enemy hopes for.

The reason you were attacked in your youth (or adult life) is because you are so great! The enemy knows just how wonderful you are; he just hopes you never catch on. One of my favorite passages in the Bible is **Philippians 1:6, "Being confident of this very thing, that He which hath begun a good work in you will perform it until the day of Jesus Christ."** Let me encourage you to be confident in the God that created you. You are something special. When He created you, He looked at you and saw it was good!!!

P.S.

I'm doing well! God is a healer!! I no longer have those attacks I had when I was first diagnosed with Multiple Sclerosis. God is **Jehovah Rapha** (The healing God)! He can heal you too; even your broken heart. I want you to believe it!!

Psalms 34:18-20 states, "The righteous cry out, and the Lord hears them; he delivers them from all their troubles. The Lord is close to the brokenhearted and saves those who are crushed in spirit. The righteous person may have many troubles, but the Lord delivers him from them all; he protects all his bones, not one of them will be broken."

Be Blessed,
Shawnte M. Mckinnon

I'VE GOT TO COMB MY HAIR

In reading this book, I hope you find that obstacles will always be present in your life, but you determine the outcome in which you allow these obstacles to affect you. I've placed a few note pages in the back of this book for you to jot down some notes about the obstacles in your own journey and what steps you are going take to overcome them. It is not by chance that you've read this book. I was placed on assignment to write this book specifically for you. It's time for you to heal! Remember, all things are possible with God!

I'VE GOT TO COMB MY HAIR

I'VE GOT TO COMB MY HAIR

NOTES

I'VE GOT TO COMB MY HAIR

NOTES

I'VE GOT TO COMB MY HAIR

NOTES

I'VE GOT TO COMB MY HAIR

NOTES

I'VE GOT TO COMB MY HAIR

NOTES

I'VE GOT TO COMB MY HAIR

Contact Shawnte

Website: www.shawntemckinnon.com

Email: info@shawntemckinnon.com

Facebook: https://www.facebook.com/shawnte.mckinnon

Made in the USA
Columbia, SC
23 February 2022